This planner belongs to:

_____

Calendar

2 0 2 3

January

Mo	Tu	We	Th	Fr	Sa	Su
						1
2	3	4	5	6	7	8
9	10	11	12	13	14	15
16	17	18	19	20	21	22
23	24	25	26	27	28	29
30	31					

February

Mo	Tu	We	Th	Fr	Sa	Su
		1	2	3	4	5
6	7	8	9	10	11	12
13	14	15	16	17	18	19
20	21	22	23	24	25	26
27	28					

March

Mo	Tu	We	Th	Fr	Sa	Su
		1	2	3	4	5
6	7	8	9	10	11	12
13	14	15	16	17	18	19
20	21	22	23	24	25	26
27	28	29	30	31		

April

Mo	Tu	We	Th	Fr	Sa	Su
					1	2
3	4	5	6	7	8	9
10	11	12	13	14	15	16
17	18	19	20	21	22	23
24	25	26	27	28	29	30

May

Mo	Tu	We	Th	Fr	Sa	Su
1	2	3	4	5	6	7
8	9	10	11	12	13	14
15	16	17	18	19	20	21
22	23	24	25	26	27	28
29	30	31				

June

Mo	Tu	We	Th	Fr	Sa	Su
			1	2	3	4
5	6	7	8	9	10	11
12	13	14	15	16	17	18
19	20	21	22	23	24	25
26	27	28	29	30		

July

Mo	Tu	We	Th	Fr	Sa	Su
					1	2
3	4	5	6	7	8	9
10	11	12	13	14	15	16
17	18	19	20	21	22	23
24	25	26	27	28	29	30
31						

August

Mo	Tu	We	Th	Fr	Sa	Su
	1	2	3	4	5	6
7	8	9	10	11	12	13
14	15	16	17	18	19	20
21	22	23	24	25	26	27
28	29	30	31			

September

Mo	Tu	We	Th	Fr	Sa	Su
				1	2	3
4	5	6	7	8	9	10
11	12	13	14	15	16	17
18	19	20	21	22	23	24
25	26	27	28	29	30	

October

Mo	Tu	We	Th	Fr	Sa	Su
						1
2	3	4	5	6	7	8
9	10	11	12	13	14	15
16	17	18	19	20	21	22
23	24	25	26	27	28	29
30	31					

November

Mo	Tu	We	Th	Fr	Sa	Su
		1	2	3	4	5
6	7	8	9	10	11	12
13	14	15	16	17	18	19
20	21	22	23	24	25	26
27	28	29	30			

December

Mo	Tu	We	Th	Fr	Sa	Su
				1	2	3
4	5	6	7	8	9	10
11	12	13	14	15	16	17
18	19	20	21	22	23	24
25	26	27	28	29	30	31

Calendar

2024

January

Mo	Tu	We	Th	Fr	Sa	Su
1	2	3	4	5	6	7
8	9	10	11	12	13	14
15	16	17	18	19	20	21
22	23	24	25	26	27	28
29	30	31				

February

Mo	Tu	We	Th	Fr	Sa	Su
			1	2	3	4
5	6	7	8	9	10	11
12	13	14	15	16	17	18
19	20	21	22	23	24	25
26	27	28	29			

March

Mo	Tu	We	Th	Fr	Sa	Su
				1	2	3
4	5	6	7	8	9	10
11	12	13	14	15	16	17
18	19	20	21	22	23	24
25	26	27	28	29	30	31

April

Mo	Tu	We	Th	Fr	Sa	Su
1	2	3	4	5	6	7
8	9	10	11	12	13	14
15	16	17	18	19	20	21
22	23	24	25	26	27	28
29	30					

May

Mo	Tu	We	Th	Fr	Sa	Su
		1	2	3	4	5
6	7	8	9	10	11	12
13	14	15	16	17	18	19
20	21	22	23	24	25	26
27	28	29	30	31		

June

Mo	Tu	We	Th	Fr	Sa	Su
					1	2
3	4	5	6	7	8	9
10	11	12	13	14	15	16
17	18	19	20	21	22	23
24	25	26	27	28	29	30

July

Mo	Tu	We	Th	Fr	Sa	Su
1	2	3	4	5	6	7
8	9	10	11	12	13	14
15	16	17	18	19	20	21
22	23	24	25	26	27	28
29	30	31				

August

Mo	Tu	We	Th	Fr	Sa	Su
			1	2	3	4
5	6	7	8	9	10	11
12	13	14	15	16	17	18
19	20	21	22	23	24	25
26	27	28	29	30	31	

September

Mo	Tu	We	Th	Fr	Sa	Su
						1
2	3	4	5	6	7	8
9	10	11	12	13	14	15
16	17	18	19	20	21	22
23	24	25	26	27	28	29
30						

October

Mo	Tu	We	Th	Fr	Sa	Su
	1	2	3	4	5	6
7	8	9	10	11	12	13
14	15	16	17	18	19	20
21	22	23	24	25	26	27
28	29	30	31			

November

Mo	Tu	We	Th	Fr	Sa	Su
				1	2	3
4	5	6	7	8	9	10
11	12	13	14	15	16	17
18	19	20	21	22	23	24
25	26	27	28	29	30	

December

Mo	Tu	We	Th	Fr	Sa	Su
						1
2	3	4	5	6	7	8
9	10	11	12	13	14	15
16	17	18	19	20	21	22
23	24	25	26	27	28	29
30	31					

I can and I will

Health

Family

Relationships

Career

Personal

my vision board

vision board

vision board

Goal Planner

Goal 1

Action plans

_____

_____

_____

_____

_____

Goal 2

Action plans

_____

_____

_____

_____

_____

Goal 3

Action plans

_____

_____

_____

_____

_____

Total Income: **Total Expenses:**   **Difference:**

Fixed Expenses	Amount	Due	Other Expenses	Amount	Due

Savings Tracker			Debt Tracker		
Beginning Balance	This Month	Year to Date	Beginning Balance	This Month:	Year to Date

Total Income: **Total Expenses:**   **Difference:**

Fixed Expenses	Amount	Due	Other Expenses	Amount	Due

Savings Tracker

Beginning Balance	This Month	Year to Date

Debt Tracker

Beginning Balance	This Month:	Year to Date

Daily
IncomeTracker

DATE	INCOME	EXPENSES	PRODUCTS	OTHER	TOTAL

TOTAL	REVENUE	EXPENSES	PRODUCTS	OTHERS	GROSS TOTAL

Daily
IncomeTracker

DATE	INCOME	EXPENSES	PRODUCTS	OTHER	TOTAL
TOTAL	REVENUE	EXPENSES	PRODUCTS	OTHERS	GROSS TOTAL

monthly budget

Total Income: **Total Expenses:**   **Difference:**

Fixed Expenses	Amount	Due	Other Expenses	Amount	Due

Savings Tracker

Beginning Balance	This Month	Year to Date

Debt Tracker

Beginning Balance	This Month:	Year to Date

monthly **budget**

Total Income: **Total Expenses:**   **Difference:**

Fixed Expenses	Amount	Due	Other Expenses	Amount	Due

Savings Tracker		
Beginning Balance	This Month	Year to Date

Debt Tracker		
Beginning Balance	This Month:	Year to Date

Daily
IncomeTracker

DATE	INCOME	EXPENSES	PRODUCTS	OTHER	TOTAL

TOTAL	REVENUE	EXPENSES	PRODUCTS	OTHERS	GROSS TOTAL

Daily
IncomeTracker

DATE	INCOME	EXPENSES	PRODUCTS	OTHER	TOTAL

TOTAL	REVENUE	EXPENSES	PRODUCTS	OTHERS	GROSS TOTAL

monthly
budget

Total Income: **Total Expenses:**   **Difference:**

Fixed Expenses	Amount	Due	Other Expenses	Amount	Due

Savings Tracker		
Beginning Balance	This Month	Year to Date

Debt Tracker		
Beginning Balance	This Month:	Year to Date

Total Income: **Total Expenses:**   **Difference:**

Fixed Expenses	Amount	Due	Other Expenses	Amount	Due

Savings Tracker

Beginning Balance	This Month	Year to Date

Debt Tracker

Beginning Balance	This Month:	Year to Date

Daily
IncomeTracker

DATE	INCOME	EXPENSES	PRODUCTS	OTHER	TOTAL
TOTAL	REVENUE	EXPENSES	PRODUCTS	OTHERS	GROSS TOTAL

Daily
IncomeTracker

DATE	INCOME	EXPENSES	PRODUCTS	OTHER	TOTAL
TOTAL	REVENUE	EXPENSES	PRODUCTS	OTHERS	GROSS TOTAL

monthly
budget

Total Income: | **Total Expenses:** | **Difference:**

Fixed Expenses	Amount	Due	Other Expenses	Amount	Due

Savings Tracker		
Beginning Balance	This Month	Year to Date

Debt Tracker		
Beginning Balance	This Month:	Year to Date

Total Income: **Total Expenses:**   **Difference:**

Fixed Expenses	Amount	Due	Other Expenses	Amount	Due

Savings Tracker		
Beginning Balance	This Month	Year to Date

Debt Tracker		
Beginning Balance	This Month:	Year to Date

Daily
IncomeTracker

DATE	INCOME	EXPENSES	PRODUCTS	OTHER	TOTAL
TOTAL	REVENUE	EXPENSES	PRODUCTS	OTHERS	GROSS TOTAL

Daily
IncomeTracker

DATE	INCOME	EXPENSES	PRODUCTS	OTHER	TOTAL
TOTAL	REVENUE	EXPENSES	PRODUCTS	OTHERS	GROSS TOTAL

Goal Planner

Goal 1

Action plans

_____

_____

_____

_____

_____

Goal 2

Action plans

_____

_____

_____

_____

Goal 3

Action plans

_____

_____

_____

_____

_____

monthly
budget

Total Income:　　　　**Total Expenses:**　　　　**Difference:**

Fixed Expenses	Amount	Due	Other Expenses	Amount	Due

Savings Tracker		
Beginning Balance	This Month	Year to Date

Debt Tracker		
Beginning Balance	This Month:	Year to Date

monthly
budget

Total Income: **Total Expenses:**   **Difference:**

Fixed Expenses	Amount	Due	Other Expenses	Amount	Due

Savings Tracker				Debt Tracker		
Beginning Balance	This Month	Year to Date		Beginning Balance	This Month:	Year to Date

Daily
IncomeTracker

DATE	INCOME	EXPENSES	PRODUCTS	OTHER	TOTAL

TOTAL	REVENUE	EXPENSES	PRODUCTS	OTHERS	GROSS TOTAL

Daily
IncomeTracker

DATE	INCOME	EXPENSES	PRODUCTS	OTHER	TOTAL
TOTAL	REVENUE	EXPENSES	PRODUCTS	OTHERS	GROSS TOTAL

monthly
budget

Total Income: **Total Expenses:**   **Difference:**

Fixed Expenses	Amount	Due	Other Expenses	Amount	Due

Savings Tracker			Debt Tracker		
Beginning Balance	This Month	Year to Date	Beginning Balance	This Month:	Year to Date

Daily
IncomeTracker

DATE	INCOME	EXPENSES	PRODUCTS	OTHER	TOTAL

TOTAL	REVENUE	EXPENSES	PRODUCTS	OTHERS	GROSS TOTAL

Daily
IncomeTracker

DATE	INCOME	EXPENSES	PRODUCTS	OTHER	TOTAL

TOTAL	REVENUE	EXPENSES	PRODUCTS	OTHERS	GROSS TOTAL

monthly
budget

Total Income: **Total Expenses:**   **Difference:**

Fixed Expenses	Amount	Due	Other Expenses	Amount	Due

Savings Tracker

Beginning Balance	This Month	Year to Date

Debt Tracker

Beginning Balance	This Month:	Year to Date

monthly
budget

Total Income: **Total Expenses:**   **Difference:**

Fixed Expenses	Amount	Due	Other Expenses	Amount	Due

Savings Tracker		
Beginning Balance	This Month	Year to Date

Debt Tracker		
Beginning Balance	This Month:	Year to Date

Daily
IncomeTracker

DATE	INCOME	EXPENSES	PRODUCTS	OTHER	TOTAL

TOTAL	REVENUE	EXPENSES	PRODUCTS	OTHERS	GROSS TOTAL

Daily Income Tracker

DATE	INCOME	EXPENSES	PRODUCTS	OTHER	TOTAL

TOTAL	REVENUE	EXPENSES	PRODUCTS	OTHERS	GROSS TOTAL

Total Income:　　　　**Total Expenses:**　　　　**Difference:**

Fixed Expenses	Amount	Due	Other Expenses	Amount	Due

Savings Tracker

Beginning Balance	This Month	Year to Date

Debt Tracker

Beginning Balance	This Month:	Year to Date

monthly
budget

Total Income: **Total Expenses:**   **Difference:**

Fixed Expenses	Amount	Due	Other Expenses	Amount	Due

Savings Tracker			Debt Tracker		
Beginning Balance	This Month	Year to Date	Beginning Balance	This Month:	Year to Date

Daily
IncomeTracker

DATE	INCOME	EXPENSES	PRODUCTS	OTHER	TOTAL
TOTAL	REVENUE	EXPENSES	PRODUCTS	OTHERS	GROSS TOTAL

Daily Income Tracker

DATE	INCOME	EXPENSES	PRODUCTS	OTHER	TOTAL

TOTAL	REVENUE	EXPENSES	PRODUCTS	OTHERS	GROSS TOTAL

Goal Planner

Goal 1

Action plans

_____

_____

_____

_____

_____

Goal 2

Action plans

_____

_____

_____

_____

_____

Goal 3

Action plans

_____

_____

_____

_____

_____

Total Income: **Total Expenses:**   **Difference:**

Fixed Expenses	Amount	Due	Other Expenses	Amount	Due

Savings Tracker		
Beginning Balance	This Month	Year to Date

Debt Tracker		
Beginning Balance	This Month:	Year to Date

Total Income:　　　　**Total Expenses:**　　　　**Difference:**

Fixed Expenses	Amount	Due	Other Expenses	Amount	Due

Savings Tracker

Beginning Balance	This Month	Year to Date

Debt Tracker

Beginning Balance	This Month:	Year to Date

Daily
IncomeTracker

DATE	INCOME	EXPENSES	PRODUCTS	OTHER	TOTAL

TOTAL	REVENUE	EXPENSES	PRODUCTS	OTHERS	GROSS TOTAL

Daily IncomeTracker

DATE	INCOME	EXPENSES	PRODUCTS	OTHER	TOTAL
TOTAL	REVENUE	EXPENSES	PRODUCTS	OTHERS	GROSS TOTAL

Total Income: **Total Expenses:**   **Difference:**

Fixed Expenses	Amount	Due	Other Expenses	Amount	Due

Savings Tracker		
Beginning Balance	This Month	Year to Date

Debt Tracker		
Beginning Balance	This Month:	Year to Date

monthly
budget

Total Income:		Total Expenses:		Difference:	

Fixed Expenses	Amount	Due	Other Expenses	Amount	Due

Savings Tracker		
Beginning Balance	This Month	Year to Date

Debt Tracker		
Beginning Balance	This Month:	Year to Date

Daily IncomeTracker

DATE	INCOME	EXPENSES	PRODUCTS	OTHER	TOTAL

TOTAL	REVENUE	EXPENSES	PRODUCTS	OTHERS	GROSS TOTAL

Daily Income Tracker

DATE	INCOME	EXPENSES	PRODUCTS	OTHER	TOTAL
TOTAL	REVENUE	EXPENSES	PRODUCTS	OTHERS	GROSS TOTAL

Goal Planner

Goal 1

Action plans

_____

_____

_____

_____

_____

Goal 2

Action plans

_____

_____

_____

_____

_____

Goal 3

Action plans

_____

_____

_____

_____

_____

Savings Tracker

Saving for	Amount	Due by

DATE	WITHDRAWAL	DEPOSIT	BALANCE
		TOTAL SAVINGS	

Savings Tracker

Saving for _____   Amount _____   Due by _____

DATE	WITHDRAWAL	DEPOSIT	BALANCE
		TOTAL SAVINGS	

Savings Tracker

Saving for _____ Amount _____ Due by _____

DATE	WITHDRAWAL	DEPOSIT	BALANCE
		TOTAL SAVINGS	

Savings Tracker

Saving for	Amount	Due by

DATE	WITHDRAWAL	DEPOSIT	BALANCE
		TOTAL SAVINGS	

Savings Tracker

Saving for	Amount	Due by

DATE	WITHDRAWAL	DEPOSIT	BALANCE
		TOTAL SAVINGS	

Savings Goal Tracker

Goal Amount: _____

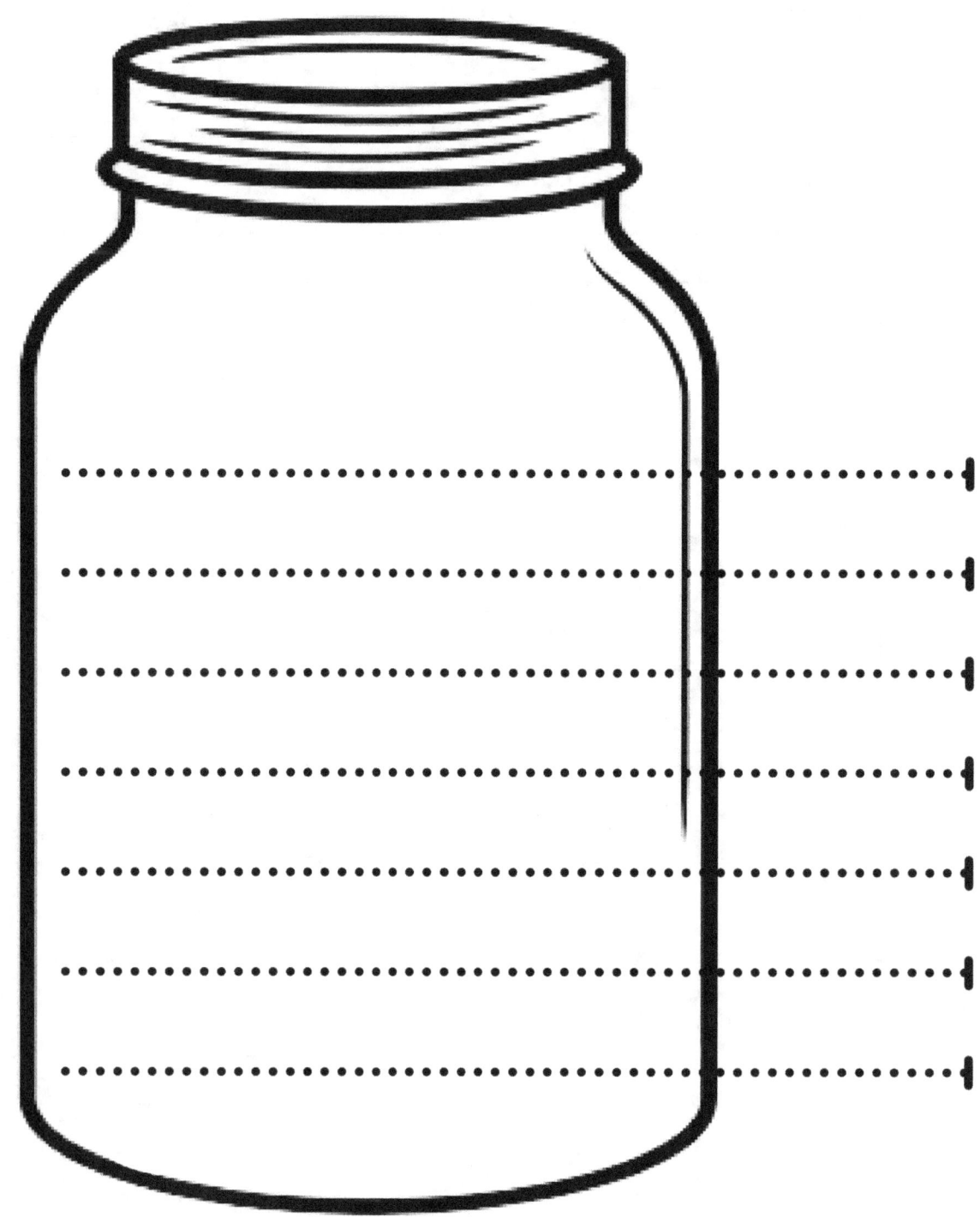

Savings Goal Tracker

Goal Amount: _____

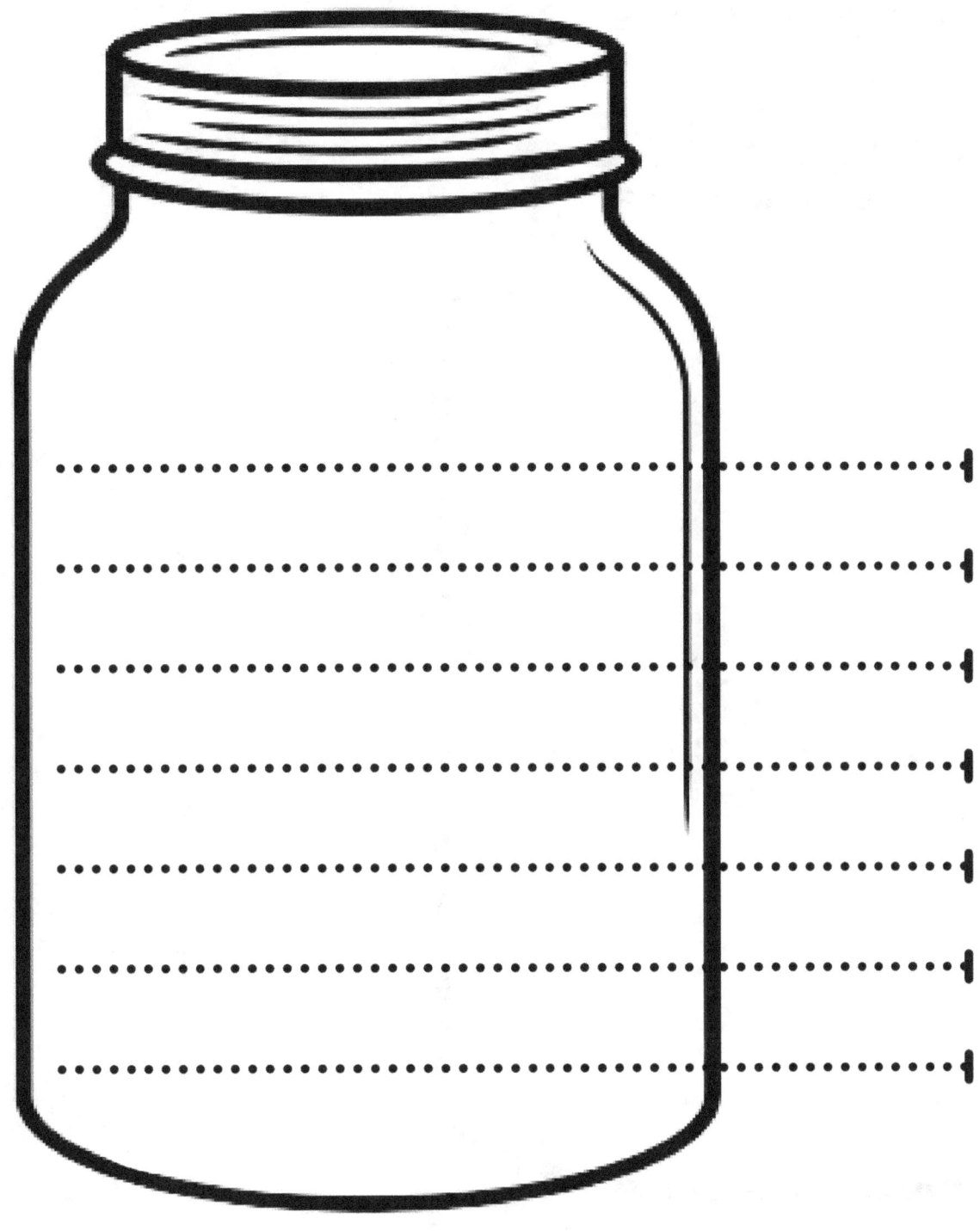

Savings Goal Tracker

Goal Amount: _____

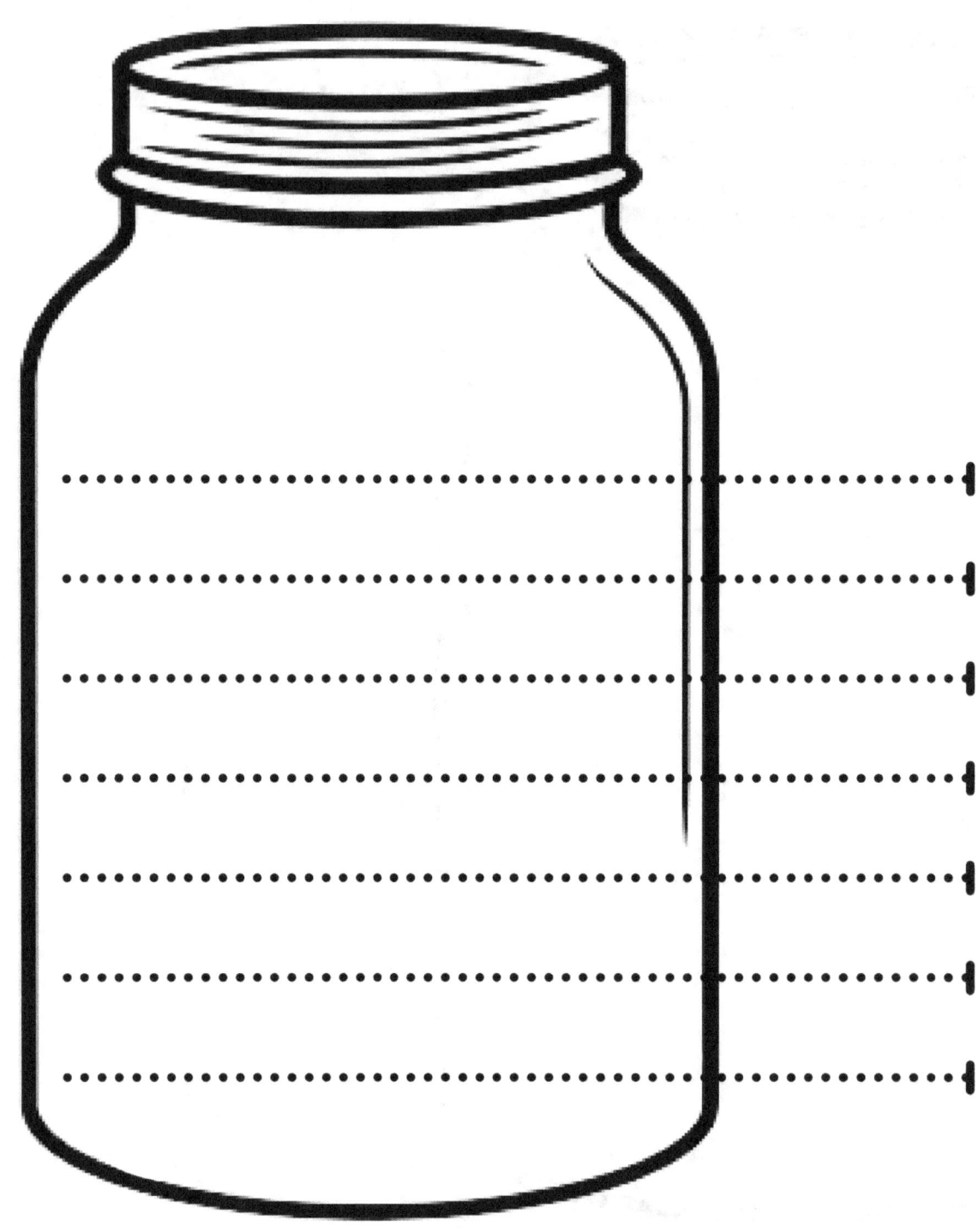

Savings Goal Tracker

Goal Amount: _____

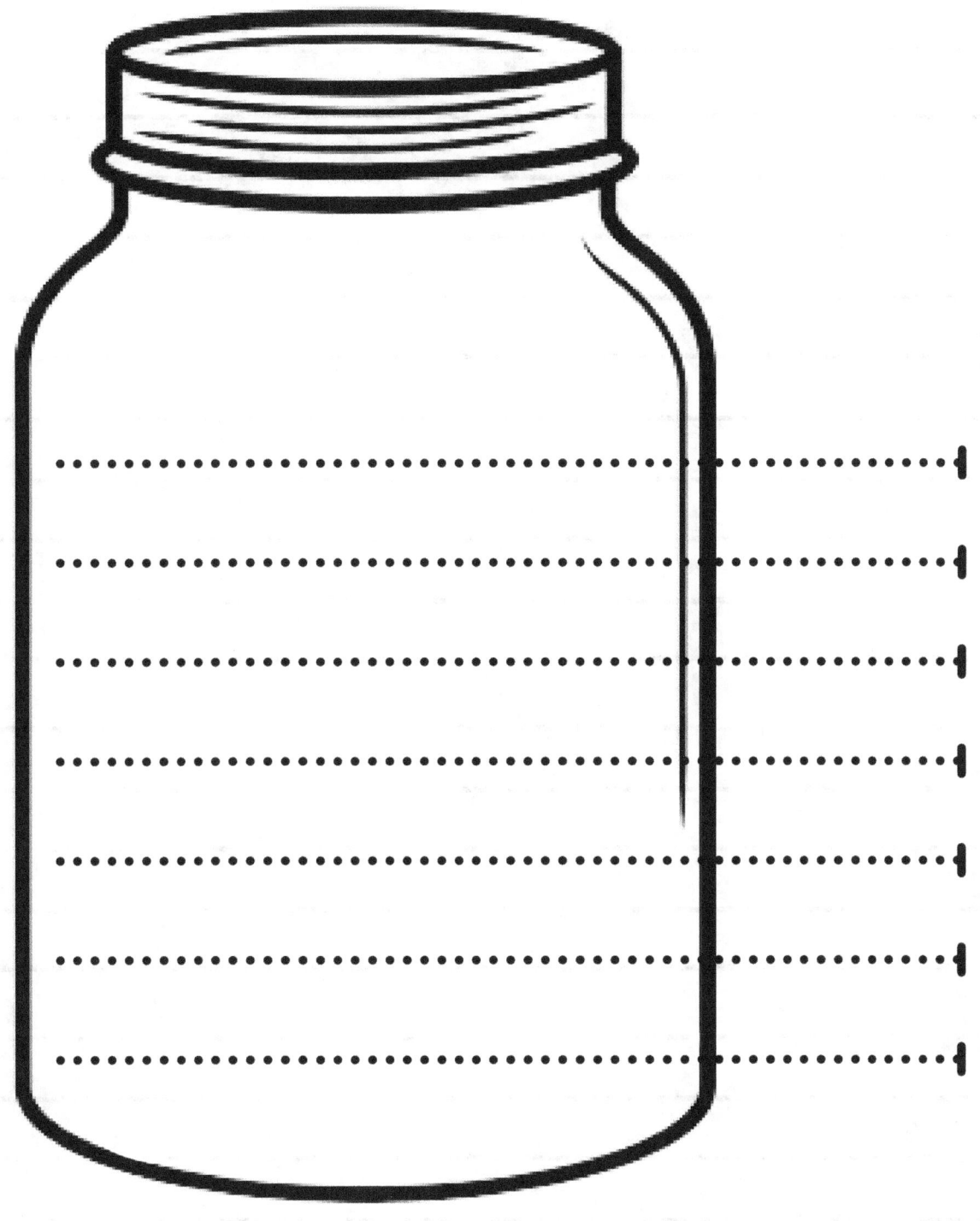

www.ingramcontent.com/pod-product-compliance
Lightning Source LLC
Chambersburg PA
CBHW080825170526

45158CB00009B/2524